Dark Psychology

The Power of Persuasion & Manipulation

by

Sebastian Goff

© Copyright 2017 by Sebastian Goff - All rights reserved.

The follow eBook is reproduced below with the goal of providing information that is as accurate and reliable as possible. Regardless, purchasing this eBook can be seen as consent to the fact that both the publisher and the author of this book are in no way experts on the topics discussed within and that any recommendations or suggestions that are made herein are for entertainment purposes only. Professionals should be consulted as needed prior to undertaking any of the action endorsed herein.

This declaration is deemed fair and valid by both the American Bar Association and the Committee of Publishers Association and is legally binding throughout the United States.

Furthermore, the transmission, duplication or reproduction of any of the following work including specific information will be considered an illegal act irrespective of if it is done electronically or in print. This extends to creating a secondary or tertiary copy of the work or a recorded copy and is only allowed with express written consent from the Publisher. All additional right reserved.

The information in the following pages is broadly considered to be a truthful and accurate account of facts and as such any inattention, use or misuse of the information in question by the reader will render any resulting actions solely under their purview. There are no scenarios in which the publisher or the original author of this work can be in any fashion deemed liable for any hardship or damages that may befall them after undertaking information described herein.

Additionally, the information in the following pages is intended only for informational purposes and should thus be thought of as universal. As befitting its nature, it is presented without assurance regarding its prolonged validity or interim quality. Trademarks that are mentioned are done without written consent and can in no way be considered an endorsement from the trademark holder.

Contents

Introduction 5

Chapter 1 – The Power of Persuasion 9

Chapter 2 - The Make-up of a Manipulator 21

Chapter 3 - Mind Control and Ethics 35

Chapter 4 - Subliminal influencing: Persuasion You're Not Aware of 49

Chapter 5 - Brainwashing 69

Chapter 6 - The Most Powerful Mind-Power Tool 89

Chapter 7 – Mind Control Techniques and Your Career 99

Chapter 8 - Mind Control in Love & Relationships 117

Conclusion 127

Introduction

Manipulation is the subtle art of getting someone to do what you want, that they would otherwise not do if asked directly. Like any other art, it is something that can be learned and improved upon with practice.

While manipulation entails a certain amount of deception, it doesn't necessarily mean that the manipulator wants to harm their target. Most of the time they just want to influence them for some personal gain, whether emotionally, financially, physically or even sexually.

Although the term manipulation carries a certain stigma, we're all guilty of manipulating each other. It doesn't always mean we don't like each other, it's simply a game of power and control.

Persuasion is regarded as a 'soft' influential technique that is used in politics, sales, negotiations, relationships and in any dealings with other people. Therefore, it is incredibly useful. The most basic skill that manipulators possess, is the ability to effectively read other peoples emotional and mental state.

Skilled manipulators know how to deceive through understanding the psychological vulnerabilities of their victims. They achieve this by successfully concealing their real intentions. This enables them to choose the best manipulation tactic, for each and every vulnerability they expose. In this book you will learn how to do this!

We tend to believe manipulators must possess a certain degree of ruthlessness and to feel sorry for the harm they cause their victims. This is the picture which is painted by movies and TV soap operas. But the reality is anyone can manipulate and persuade others, even the nicest people you know!

This book will show you how the world we live in is manipulating the way we see and perceive things. You may ask yourself if it's possible to be manipulated by the TV shows you watch? This book will give you these answers.

There is also a chapter on Brainwashing, where someone's beliefs and opinions about something are radically changed by the use of systematic or forcible methods. This can even occur in our closet relationships, we are sometimes made to believe we're not good enough, pretty enough, or smart enough.

Different persuasion techniques have been used throughout the ages. A well-known 17th-century French physicist and philosopher, Blaise Pascal, claimed that the guaranteed way of persuading someone to do what you want is not by bombarding them with your ideas, but by 'slipping in through the backdoor of their beliefs'. In other words, persuasion through smarts and sweetness, not authority.

Pascal is well-known for his ideas that eloquence is an art of saying things in such a way that those to whom you speak may listen without feeling hurt or belittled but feel happy to accept your ideas as their own.

With the ability to influence we become much more powerful in life and therefore get more of our needs met. But, first be clear about what you want to achieve and then work out an effective strategy on how to do it.

If you're regularly involved in business or tough negotiations, the ability to read people will be by far one of your most valuable skills. Those we interact with each day send us signals, and if we can learn what to look and listen out for, each person will tell us exactly how to influence them. Reading people accurately is a skill that anyone can master by paying more attention. The easiest prey for mind manipulation are usually the over-sensitive or over-conscientious individuals.

When we want something we usually present our side of an argument with the hope the other person will be willing to agree to our request. With this option, there is a high probability they will say no. But using the information outlined in this book you can learn advanced persuasion strategies which are based upon human psychological loopholes and subconscious influencing.

This title will show you these methods outlined in clear and easy to follow ways. By understanding what motivates us, we can use these basic human needs as leverage to get people to say 'Yes' to us more often. You will also find advanced NLP (Neuro-Linguistic Programming) techniques used by world-renowned magicians which are now available for you. These techniques and methods have been cleverly devised to teach you how to breeze through life while getting most of your needs met.

Please leave your morals behind, as the aim of this book is to show you the darker side of getting what you want.

Chapter 1 – The Power of Persuasion

Becoming more persuasive can help us many walks of life, from making us more efficient at our jobs or helping us attract an amazing partner to successfully debating and influencing others. The ability to persuade means we have changed someone's perception on something, which otherwise would have stayed the same. This shows just how powerful this art is. We can make people think or behave in the way we want them to - now that's magic.

Throughout history the most powerful leaders and trail blazers seemingly possessed a quality which made others believe in them and subsequently follow them. These influential people mastered the art of persuasion. They had a way of communicating which made others pay attention. Most of us have met people who have a natural sense of charm and they somehow seem to easily gain the trust of others. I believe all of us are born with this natural charisma, however due to the struggles of life we lose touch with it. In this chapter, you will learn how to get back in tune with your natural persuasive abilities.

To understand what makes people persuadable we have to learn what makes them tick first. We do this of course by looking under the hood at human psychology. Changing the way people think involves altering their attitudes, values, beliefs and goals which then impacts what action they take in the future.

Persuasion is made-up of 6 main aspects -

<u>Intent</u> – Persuasion should come across quite naturally but with intention. We want people to see our perspective on things. The 'hard sell' or aggressive tactics rarely work in this modern day and age. Most positive interactions will lead to a change in perception in both parties.

<u>Force</u> - This is when a persuasive act gains compliance from the other, so they follow the behavior you requested. However, it doesn't change their internal beliefs. It may actually strengthen their beliefs in the opposite direction. This occurs when people are forced or made to do something against their will.

<u>Context</u> - A new behavior may only be relevant within a certain context. For instance, someone may be pressured into arriving at work on time. But will continue to be late for every other appointment they have outside of work. Their

inner beliefs around punctuation haven't shifted.

<u>Plurality</u> - This means being able to persuade a number of people at one time.

<u>Presence</u> - When we persuade in person, it is deemed maximum communication since we are present physically. We can also persuade through different means such as e-mail, telephone, social media, letters etc. These methods aren't as influential as physical presence.

Our internal programming's are usually formed as a network of beliefs. The art of persuasion involves breaking and redirecting some of these connections to create a new belief. Sometimes we may have to alter a number of interconnected beliefs before we can change a deep core belief.

Basic Human Needs

From a psychological understanding we know that humans have fundamental needs. This has been defined in many texts none more so than Abraham Maslow's hierarchy of needs. Using this model major corporations and advertising agencies have been able to determine what appeals to the most basic of human needs, so they can increase interest in or sell a particular product. The main emotions these companies focus upon is Safety, Belonging and Esteem (well-being). Since these are basic needs it makes them powerful motivators for advertisers to use. These three emotions are ranked highly in most people's personal value structure. In fact, the more these needs are fulfilled the more happiness and peace we experience in life.

So, by creating a sense of safety, belonging or making people feel important, we open the doors to influencing and persuasion. Here are three simple phrases which help change the way we see things -

1) 'What if' - This phrase takes ego out of the equation and allows people to feel comfortable in creating a safe environment where they can explore deeper feelings and curiosities. 'What if' is a magical phrase and we often hear it from children when they allow their imaginations to run wild. Used wisely it can be leveraged to open people's minds to new ideas and possibilities. Try asking someone, 'what if you had a million dollars?', they'll tell you more about their real desires and interests than you may have known prior.

2) 'Can you help please?' - This phrase intentionally hands the power to the opposite party. Humans naturally want to help others. By using this statement consciously, we can rely on people's good nature to get us what we want.

3) 'Would it help if' - Similar to example 1, such a statement shifts the focus from a problem to a solution. At the same time using the word 'if', allows the interaction or suggestion to maintain some flexibility. Most of us don't like doing things another person's way but by using the word 'if' we can gradually get others to accept our proposal.

The above three powerful phrases can also work effectively in emails and letters. Simply try using one of these phrases as your email header in the subject line next time you're messaging someone and see how they work for you.

Dale Carnegie the famous author of the book 'How to Win Friends & Influence People' discussed the art of influencing others at great depth. Here is a snippet of some of his main points to winning people over.

1 - The only way to win an argument is to avoid it.
2 - Respect other people's opinions. Be open minded and never say, 'You're wrong.'
3 - If however, you're wrong, don't be afraid of admitting it quickly and emphatically.
4 - Always start an interaction in a friendly way.
5 - Get the opposite party agreeing with you immediately by getting them saying "yes, yes, yes".

6 - Listen intently. Let the other person do most of the talking.

7 - Allow the other person to feel that an idea or suggestion come from them.

8 - Use empathy to see things from the other person's stand point. Acknowledging this perspective, gives us greater power.

9 - Show understanding and sympathy for the other people's ideas and needs.

10 - Make things easier by appealing to people's values and motives.

11 - Set challenges for others. Competitive people naturally welcome challenges. Use this to your advantage.

Social - Being Liked

Sociality has a huge impact upon how easily people are influenced. Social proof means how well we are accepted by people and groups, whether personal or professional. How we are influenced in social situations is through three main factors - authority, likability and social proof. We are influenced by authority figures, by the people we like and those who provide us with social proof. For instance, a teenager at school would gain 'social proof' if they were seen mingling with the popular crowd.

Since humans are social creatures, we want to feel connected to one another and as though we're part of something bigger. For this reason, we're more likely to do something simply because we see others doing it. For instance, in a sales negotiation, a company may show a potential new client all the other businesses in the area they deal with. Or in a one-to-one situation we can influence someone by explaining Mr. Popular from another department agreed to it. Knowing others have taken some action before us helps to naturally reduce resistance.

Authority

We're naturally more influenced by those we deem to be above us in some respect. You're more likely to follow directions when they come from management at your place of work rather than if they came from a fellow colleague. We look up too and respect those who are an expert within a certain area or subject, we see these people as an authority.

Something as simple as informing an audience or an individual of your credentials prior to an interaction can help swing the odds into your favor when looking to persuade or influence. This technique can also be effective when emailing, by simply stating at the beginning about any skills you possess in relation to the subject can help make the other person more susceptible to your influence. If for example, you were contacting someone about the possibility of speaking at their event and you had previous experience of speaking at big events, the mere mention of the biggest events you've spoken at, would have an impact on the way the recipient would view your application. We can use this too our advantage and maybe even exaggerate our accomplishments.

Consistency

This is another means of getting people to buy-in to us and is often used as a sales tactic. In this method we ask the target to admit their goals and priorities first and then align our request with their desires. This makes it difficult for them to say no too. Use the information they originally provided and offer them a solution based upon it.

People like to remain consistent and don't like being seen as dishonest, which is why it makes it harder for them to reject a request which matches their needs. When a target shares their goals first, they are invested, once they're invested we can offer the right solutions for them.

Here are a few further strategies which can be used to influence.

This method is named Disrupt and Reframe - This process involves mixing up the words, behaviors or visuals a person is used too and then reframing our pitch/request while they're still trying to figure out the disruption. This method was put to the test by researchers who sold a product giving customers two different options.

The first choice offered - $3 for 8 apples
The second option offered - 300 pennies for 8 apples
The second choice was the clear winner, selling almost twice as many apples as option 1.

This technique works because the target has less resistance to the reframe (option 2) as the brain is thrown off by the initial disruption of the unusual wording.

Storytelling

Another method of getting people onside is through story telling. This enables others to identify with us and the various aspects of our story, which helps build trust. It is important however our story contains the right plot. The three main plots for an influential story are -

1. Challenge Plot - This is the story of the underdog, the rags to riches, the person who made it through some adversity on sheer willpower.
2. Connection Plot - Another common plot, where people build a relationship which bridges a certain gap. This can be racial, cultural, class, ethnic etc.
3. Creative Plot - This is a story where someone achieves a breakthrough of some sort. Whether solving a long-lasting problem or overcoming an issue in a brand new or innovative way.

If you have any personal stories which you can make meet any of the above criteria, you should find it easier to hook people in.

2. Paradoxical Intervention

This term is simply another way of saying 'Reverse Psychology'. This is a term most of us are familiar with and has been used for years.

Reverse Psychology is a persuasion method that many of us tend to use unconsciously. It involves getting someone to do something we want by suggesting the opposite. This tactic tends to work better when our target is stressed and is making emotional decisions as opposed to thinking things through.

A simple form of reverse psychology is telling someone 'not to do X', by suggesting this we are implanting this very idea into their mind. As we know, children naturally want to do whatever they've been forbidden to do. We can take this further also. If someone commits to something, we can ensure they follow through by expressing doubt over what they have promised. This will make them assert themselves by completing the action in a bid to prove us wrong.

Examples of Reverse Psychology

Here are some basic examples of where we may come across reverse psychology in our day to day life -

A mother suggests to her stingy teenager son, that he can't afford to buy his sister a birthday gift. The boy reacts to this by buying his sister an expensive present.

An office worker who is fed up with a lazy colleague who doesn't pull his weight. May say 'Ok, don't help me. I don't care'. This prompts the colleague to help out.

Or the shy boy who reacts to his friends, who suggest he's not interested in girls, by asking a girl out as his prom date.

Reverse Psychology is more likely to be effective with those who have a desire for control such as rebellious teenagers or type A personalities. They feel that by going against others, they're in control. But we can expose this vulnerability for our own gain.

When someone suggests reverse psychology is being used deliberately. Then reversing the reverse can help. It certainly helps if we act indifferent to whatever decision is made.

One problem with reverse psychology is that if there are other options or alternatives to what we have suggested the person might choose something else altogether.

Chapter 2 - The Make-up of a Manipulator

Psychological manipulation is the exploitation of other people's emotions and vulnerabilities. People generally know how to protect themselves from physical attacks, but manipulators strike at their targets psychological and emotional weaknesses.

Humans are more vulnerable than we care to admit but we also have unconscious ways of protecting ourselves. This self-protection is mostly achieved through developing a positive mindset, healthy boundaries, resilience, patience, a strong character and learning to stand up for ourselves. However, these natural defenses become relaxed around the people we believe have our best interests at heart. Also, if we're going through an emotionally difficult time such as a divorce, illness, loss of job or death of a loved one, then we become much more vulnerable and open to being taken advantage of. This becomes one of the keys of successful manipulation - finding a weak point or moment of vulnerability in the target and then exploiting it.

The Art of Manipulation

Manipulation dictionary definition -

1. *'the action of manipulating something in a skillful manner'.*

2. *'the action of manipulating someone in a clever or unscrupulous way'.*

From these dictionary explanations, we see the main points are the use of the words 'skilful', and 'clever'. These words highlight the fact that Manipulation involves a certain degree of intelligence and ability. The word 'unscrupulous' points to the fact that it's something underhand or deceitful.

This is how we generally understand Manipulation; as something negative, harmful or bad. But what if you could learn how to use it to create a better life? Earn more money? Attract your dream partner? Surely it wouldn't seem so evil then?

My understanding of Manipulation is as a subtle technique of getting what we want from others willingly, even if it's something they may not normally consent to.

No one likes to feel they've been manipulated or taken advantage of, still, we all occasionally manipulate one another. At the same time, we also find it acceptable to be manipulated in certain situations, such as by politicians or salespeople for instance. We may not openly admit it but deep down we know when we've been taken advantage of. But due to evolutionary programming, most of us will generally look to see the good in others. We think to ourselves, 'of course, other people have our best interests at heart', 'of course, this salesperson wants us to buy this car because it's the best choice for us and not because he has a monthly sales quota to achieve'.

Some of us are quick to point the finger at those who use persuasion tactics to get what they want and even label them manipulators. But, then we read about the politicians who promise people one thing to get their vote, but then backtrack once they're in power and nothing much ever gets said about it. Such people don't experience the same sort of backlash for the methods they use to get what they want as Joe Bloggs in your office does.

I point this out not because manipulation occurs more often than we care to realize but because learning these skills can make us better communicators while also teachings us how to protect ourselves against been manipulated.

Skilled Manipulators

Manipulators differ in skill, ruthlessness and the methods they use. But what they all have in common is the ability to penetrate the psychology of others.

Skilled manipulators not only know how to spot psychological weaknesses or the secret ambitions of those they target, but they also know how to use these insights to stir people into action so that they can gain something.

This subtle art involves being able to play with people's feelings and weaknesses in such a way that they often don't understand what's happening until it's too late. Manipulators develop such a mindset, that the moment they get into a new situation, whether socially or professionally, they immediately start assessing people for their value, usability, and vulnerabilities. Once a 'suitable' individual is identified, the manipulator will start analyzing their body language, facial impressions, mannerisms, vocabulary and any other subtle signs – which all lead to an assessment of the personality and character of the individual. After they've narrowed down their choice of whom to focus on, they'll work to create a relationship or closer bond. They analyze their victims until they know what makes them tick and when their victim trusts them enough to gladly accept their suggestions, they then go for the jugular.

The general tactic is to appear likable, trustworthy and friendly, usually by showing a high degree of empathy and understanding. When we show interest in people, it naturally lowers their defenses.

Kin Hubbard describes this stage very well, 'The fellow that agrees with everything you say is either a fool or he is getting ready to skin you'.

Exploiting Others' Vulnerabilities

Many of us can feel vulnerable for any number of reasons – a lack of resources, disadvantaged social status, physical disabilities, language barriers, culture and so on. In a work setting, we may find ourselves vulnerable if we're new, less experienced or less educated than others. In a social environment, one can be left feeling exposed because of their economic status, their family or educational background. In interpersonal relationships, one can be vulnerable if they come from a different culture or background, or if they have a physical disability, or maybe a less accepted sexual or religious orientation. In some cultures, unmarried or divorced women are vulnerable.

The key difference between skilled manipulation and the more extreme methods, such as brainwashing, blackmailing, bribery or racketeering, is that manipulators have a 'softer' approach and don't openly confront their victims with aggressive threats or excessive demands. This is what makes them so deadly. It's easy to protect yourself when you know who the enemy is, but in the case of manipulation, the offender is often a friend or someone you thought you could trust. This makes it easier for the victim to be lead into some falsehood.

Some people unknowingly attract manipulators, acting almost as a magnet. These are usually very naive, neurotic or insecure individuals. This is not to judge such people but with them, flattery, guilt or shame games can usually yield quick results.

Basic Manipulative Behaviors

1 - Using Your Words against you

This is a common method used by most people not just manipulators. It is also an incredibly powerful sales technique. By simply asking someone the right questions, we can gain a golden nugget of information which can then be used against them at a later point. In the case of a sales negotiation, a salesman may have uncovered your real motive behind making a purchase, this might be that you need a new car so you can travel to see your family on weekends. Once the salesperson knows your real buying motive, he can literally beat you to death with it until you agree to the sale. It can be difficult to argue against something which is true, which is why arguments are best won if we use reasons people give us against them. We could say 'you said this.....', or 'you did this...', by repeatedly highlighting the other person's actual behavior or words it traps them from overcoming our side of the argument.

2 - Refuse to be held accountable

Manipulators may simply lie and twist truths when it suits them to get out of disagreements or arguments. But their skill lies in the level of conviction they use to spin these lies. They tell these untruths in such a way they actually believe what they're saying.

3 - Blame

Emotional manipulators will try to move away from taking responsibility for a mistake. Rather they'll look to shift the blame onto a susceptible or weaker person. They may often play the victim card to make other people feel guilty. If they want to gain something from you, they may try to make you feel sympathy for their plight so you justify to yourself your reasons for helping or supporting them.

Exploiting people comes easier to some than to others. Successful manipulators often don't feel sorry for the pain they may be causing their victim. Their greatest asset, which is usually a high degree of empathy, also becomes their greatest weapon.

4 - Emotional Detachment

Emotional detachment can be a highly desirable skill for a manipulator. It sometimes stems from psychological trauma usually in childhood. This is often called emotional numbing, dissociation or emotional blunting and is considered 'unhealthy' since it is a complete disconnection from the emotions. It develops as a result of childhood trauma to help the child avoid feeling painful or hurtful emotions. Unfortunately, when these children grow up into adults they often bring this programming with them.

Those who are natural manipulators probably have been subjected to such trauma which has lead to a numbing of their emotions and feelings.

Basic Manipulation Techniques

We're all guilty of playing tricks on others from time to time but they're usually quite harmless. Most of these would fall under the category of 'Basic' manipulation skills. Whereas a higher skilled manipulator would use more advanced methods to covertly influence. We tend to use less sophisticated methods in our everyday lives to get our needs met. Most of the time we're not even aware we're being manipulative.

There are many ways in which people can be coerced or forced into doing things they don't want to do, the most common methods include: guilt tripping, complaining, lying, denying, feigning ignorance or innocence, blaming, bribery, undermining, mind games, emotional blackmail, evasiveness, fake concern, apologies, flattery, gifts, and favors – as you can see that's a long list. If we're honest with ourselves, most of us have used a few of these methods more than once. This isn't to suggest we're evil or sinister people but just shows how common these methods.

Lines such as, 'After all I've done for you...', or 'If your parents ever found out about this...', or 'There's no one in the office who could do this as well as you....', are just some of the most common phrases used to make someone feel guilty or obliged to do what is asked.

Here we will consider some basic strategies which are easy to learn and apply.

Basic influential Techniques

Get your ideas into someone else's head

Make the target feel relaxed in your company. People are easily influenced when they're in an alpha state of mind, being calm and quiet promotes this state.

By paying close attention to your words and tonality you can lure people into relaxed states more easily. Observe if your words and tonality are having the desired effect on your targets physiology, posture and body language. Practice this with close relatives and friends, notice how they naturally relax or become excited based on how you communicate with them. Raising the voice or speaking quickly naturally gets people more alert, whereas speaking slower and quietly tends to have a more relaxing effect. Also pay attention to people's eyes, here we can usually see the first signs relaxation as the pupils naturally dilate and get larger.

You can pay even closer attention by looking to see if the pulse in the neck is beating fast or slow. This requires practice, but it can further help determine how the opposite party is feeling.

Breathing patterns also change in relation to the state of mind of an individual. When we are relaxed we tend to breath more deeply otherwise known as 'belly breathing' but when overwhelmed or stressed the breathing tends to be shallower.
If you can get someone feeling relaxed (large pupils), calm (breathing slowly and deeply) and safe in your company (open body posture), this is when they'll be most susceptible to your influence.

Use Hot Words

'Hot words' effectively bring out emotions in people. They are most often used in sales and politics; however, they can also be successfully used in everyday conversations to influence or persuade.

These words may seem ordinary at first, but they're actually very suggestive because of their connection to the senses, words such as - hear this, see that, feel free, imagine etc. The power of such words can instantly invoke a certain state of mind through psychological short-circuiting.

By listening carefully to someone, try to figure out which hot words would have the biggest impact on them. For example, if someone often uses phrases such as "I really don't see where the problem is" or "I don't see the purpose of...". These are visual learners who's thought process is based on what they can envision (see). You can best reach visual types by using phrases such as "See it this way...", or "Look at it from another angle".

On the other hand, if someone speaks in a way such as, "I feel they were wrong..." or "I feel lost". These are kinesthetic learners and understand things best through feeling. With these types, use words such as "I feel I know what you should do", or "Feel free to call me anytime...".

The other most common learning type is auditory. Listen out for people who speak using phrases such as "I like the sound of that" or "listen to your gut".

Here you're simply adapting your language and communication to match the way others are interpreting the world. This means your message is more likely to be received in the way it was intended.

But regardless of personality type, some words just hold more power than others. Salesmen and journalists are masters of communication and know how to use the right words at the right time, for instance, the word 'cash' is more powerful than the word 'money, 'beaten' is more powerful than 'assaulted', 'starving' is more powerful than 'hungry' and so on.

Humans naturally shift through information which doesn't at first appeal to them. Hot words invoke feelings, stir up emotions and create related images and thoughts in the mind. When used skillfully, they can influence a person's decisions often without you even having to suggest anything. By learning about your target, you get to understand what to say and how to say it to get a response.

8 basic steps to developing manipulation skills

- Learn to read people. Make judgments about people and then see if you're right.
- Have a pleasant appearance. Always try to look, well-groomed, clean and tidy.
- Adopt pleasant manners. Be polite, helpful, courteous and kind.
- Act friendly, or at least try to look friendly.
- Show concern, care, empathy, be a shoulder to cry on.
- Be organized. To plan a manipulation tactic, benign or complicated, you must be able to plan accordingly from A to Z, sometimes even changing tactics.
- Develop patience. Things don't always go according to plan.
- Additional qualities: ruthlessness, cunningness, emotional detachment, shrewdness.

The art of manipulation involves two main aspects: concealing your real intentions and knowing the vulnerabilities of the target.

Chapter 3 - Mind Control and Ethics

Mind control is a loosely used term which can include many things, from little tricks employed by marketers and politicians, to serious brainwashing done by some religious cults or ideological organizations. All of them use psychology to manipulate others into doing what they want.

At the root of most mind-controlling behaviors is either personal gain or the desire to control. In individuals, these motives usually stem from self-esteem issues, the desire to gain or simply out of boredom.

Knowing you're being manipulated helps give a head start, so you can understand what's happening and then come up with an adequate plan to protect one's self. Being aware of a manipulator's game destroys any chance of it working. It's like not being impressed by a magician once you understand the mechanics behind the trick. But, if we're the ones doing the manipulation keeping our true intentions secret is paramount to having the desired success and not losing face.

There are different ways of manipulating, from very complex methods which need to be planned months or years in advance, to simpler techniques which can be applied right away, most manipulation cycles look something like this:

- Find someone's weaknesses (a desire to please, lack of assertiveness, fear of confrontation, naivety)
- Exploiting this weakness
- Benefiting

Ethical Use

We can make a case for the ethical use of Mind Control. In the realm of therapy for example. If someone gives a therapist consent to take over their mind to help them overcome some psychological issue such as anxiety or depression, this is considered positive use.

If we look at hypnosis, this could be deemed a form of mind control. It seems to be ethical because it has been consented by the patient and it offers the potential for positive change.
If you're strongly opposed to mind control even if it's used for 'ethical' reasons, then maybe you need to consider the many marketing strategies and advertising techniques we're subjected to on a daily basis to influence us into purchasing a particular product. Where do we draw the line?

It is too difficult to suggest all mind control is wrong and unethical. Is hypnosis unethical if it interferes with a person's free will and makes them change their way of thinking? Or if someone is about to commit suicide but another person uses advanced levels of mind control and psychological knowledge to talk them out of it, is that unethical? At the end of the day, is there much difference if someone physically makes someone do something through brute force or if someone influences another into action via mind control? If the end result is the same, then maybe there isn't much difference.

My own opinion on the matter is that if it is used for the greater good for the people involved then perhaps it should be acceptable.

Your own moral standards will decide how far you are prepared to go, or how low you will stoop to get something. The bottom line is, ethical persons use mind control in an ethical way, and unethical persons use it in unethical ways.

Some will claim everything is manipulative. However, it is more useful to consider influence on a range. One end of the spectrum is what's deemed the positive and respectful uses which consider people's rights. But on the opposite extreme we have more destructive forces, which tend to strip an individual of their independence, identity and the ability to think or act logically.

How useful is mind control?

Mind control is getting others to give us what we want when we want it. From the child who wants his parent to buy him a puppy or the boss who wants you to work overtime on a weekend without pay, mind control can work wonders if applied correctly.

Children are master manipulators. The child may at first beg with a soft pleading voice and eyes brimming with tears, but if that doesn't work, they resort to throwing a mini tantrum. Or, he may have figured out from experience which method works best when trying to get something from his father, and which one to use with his grandparents. As you can see, mind control is quite natural and something we learn early on in our development and perfect throughout life. We use persuasion techniques all the time but their success on larger scales depends on the power and shrewdness of the user.

Advanced mind control is a skill which can be honed through experience, knowledge and regular practice. If you're willing to learn you can develop a whole arsenal of methods to have at your disposal. This is important as it is unlikely one method will work every time or be effective with everyone.

Being a good persuader is easier if you're naturally good at reading people. But even if your mind-reading skills are not great, you should at least know what methods definitely won't work. For example, threatening your boss is rarely helpful. This approach is too overt and direct, so it can easily be thwarted by the other.

But when used subtly, mind control is incredibly influential. By simply choosing the right moment when asking for a pay raise, or knowing how to ask your father if you can use his car, these seemingly little factors may decide whether or not you get the outcome you desire.

Getting others to oblige to you regardless of how inconvenient the particular favor may be to them, can help you get more from life. However, there are some basic rules to follow.

3 things to keep in mind
- <u>Know your place.</u>

Be clear about what you are trying to achieve and from whom. Threatening your boss or someone you depend on, seldom works. On the contrary, it may even backfire. Instead be tactful.

- <u>Choose the mind control method</u>

Not every method works for everyone, or in all situations. By using the wrong method, you might miss out on getting what you want and make it even harder to achieve.

- <u>Have a backup plan.</u>

This is especially important if something big is at stake. Think things through, but anticipate things going wrong and be ready with an alternative approach or backup plan. If the first method doesn't work, be prepared to quickly and discreetly (in order not to lose face) try something else.

ISIS & Mind Control

In recent times, one of the more popular instances where mind control has been reported is by the Terrorist Organization Isis (Islamic State). From the UK alone, it is reported they have managed to recruit over 1,600 people (mostly young) to join their organization. What would make people leave the comfort of their western lives to go to war torn countries to fight or engage in a world of conflict?

The rise in numbers has been seen in what's deemed 'Online grooming'. Usually this goes on for a substantial amount of time before people blindly follow the wishes of such organizations. It has been said that the real reason westerns go and join this plight is actually more to do with the advanced manipulation techniques used as opposed to the actual cause.

Brain washing vs Mind control

Brain washing is more aggressive in nature. Sometimes people have to be taken by force and be subjected to brain washing tactics. Whereas mind control is much subtler. In the ISIS example, people are more likely to be 'seduced' by a recruiter - not sexually, but emotionally. The recruiter takes the role of someone a young person looks up to, sees as a friend, a parental figure or a mentor. This is an important dynamic to create for successful mind control.

This 'friendliness' creates an illusion of choice. This makes the indoctrination by-pass the conscious ego defenses and gets to work deeper within the psyche. The recruiters work by first finding similarities with the target, maybe they're also someone who moved from the west to come and join forces with ISIS - this creates a sense of empathy, understanding and a community based on shared beliefs.

Since most people are aware of such a terrorist organization, the group have to tread carefully as to not scare away any potential new recruits. It would likely start with a soft approach of the target. In the mind control world this would be termed the 'grooming seduction phase'. This is when flattery and compliments are used heavily, with the approach of 'How can we help you?'. This initial period builds the relationship and allows the manipulators to get their 'claws' into the target. Once they reach this point, they can then use threats to prevent you from leaving such as death threats, threats on the targets family and loved ones.

In the case of ISIS, most of the young people who are recruited don't really know what they're getting themselves into. They are given just enough information which allows them to create a fantasy in their mind. They may be convinced into believing they'll become saviors of their religion or help make world peace. This belief of a heightened sense of importance can become a very powerful motive in controlling people. Its only after joining such an organization do the recruits really begin to realize that it isn't what they expected. That in reality, they're probably not going to change the world but in fact have put their lives in grave danger.

For us people who are not involved, it is easy for us to point the finger and make judgements about those involved. But on closer inspection, we must try to realize there is something going on that would make someone join such an organization. It comes down to the use of social psychology and using it to influence people's motivation, interest and curiosity. In fact, most of the people recruited are likely to be good people. People who want to make a positive difference in the world, or want to improve themselves - by playing on these tendencies the target can eventually be manipulated into a new way of thinking.

Indoctrination Tactics

A popular model used in cults and extremist groups such as ISIS is called the four-part model. This points to the fact that most people fall into one of four categories - feelers, thinkers, believers or doers. The manipulator will start by analyzing the target to see which of these groups they fall into. For example, for feelers their motives are very emotionally driven and they want to feel part of a community or a social group. But for thinkers, they will have to be approached with more intellect and be engaged in more theoretical way. Whereas believers think this is their destiny and something which offers them deeper meaning to their life. Finally, doers are more concerned with saving lives, protecting people, fighting evil and preventing oppression of people. A skilled manipulator will be able to detect the specific personality type and find a way into influencing.

The information obtained about a person's personality can then be used to shape their character in the desired way. By controlling one of these four parts of a person, we can gradually begin to shift their identity to one which suits the cause or plight we're involved with. The new identity however, will be more obedient, have less independence or freedom of choice.

ISIS for example, may at this point give you a new name. People who have been indoctrinated in this way may even begin to believe they're above fellow human beings and are being led by some higher power such as God. This is a similar thing seen in religious cults all over the world.

Social Psychology

Most of us function under what is known as fundamental attribution of error - which is deemed to be one of the most important factors within Social Psychology. It basically means that, when we try to understand what others are doing, we have a certain error where we attribute most of the behavior on their personality and them as a person while under attributing the influence of social and environmental factors which also play a part in human programming and behavior. When we look at this closer, we tend to see that ISIS recruits are generally intelligent, good people from positive backgrounds. This points to the mind control and grooming which occurred to be quite substantial.

For mind control to work successfully, it requires the target to come back on their own accord, especially during the early stages of manipulation. By hooking them in, they can be led into believing they're coming back is their own choosing and the steps they're taking is mainly their choice.

Cults such as these will usually commit the target to keep things 'to themselves' and not to tell anyone. Also, to not change their behavior much because they're aware of how most families will react. Unfortunately, if we try to talk someone out of this, it can have the opposite effect and plunge them even deeper. Using authority and fear to combat such a problem seldom works. Instead it only works to convince the target they're on the right path. The reason why some of these recruits then go on to commit horrific crimes is because they have developed a new identity. They're not themselves anymore, from a new identity we can carry out acts and not really feel as though we were there. Especially when they're supported by others with the same thinking and beliefs.

The good news is that people who are indoctrinated, can be brought back to their true identity. Providing there is no mental health issues at play and they can be separated from the group or cult they were involved with. Of course, this doesn't occur overnight, and each case is subjective.

Mind control methods

Developing these skills requires an understanding of what you're doing. Which begins by knowing what you are trying to achieve (outcome) and who the target is.

1. Most common overt mind control methods

- Pleading (making promises, being nice, asking for a favor, crying)
- Making threats (threatening to harm others, threats to kill one's self, threatening to leave, firing you from your job, ruining your reputation, losing your title etc) if a request is rejected.

2. Religious cults and sects use mind control methods to recruit, indoctrinate and keep members, some of which include

- Mind-altering drugs
- Indoctrination with constant repetition and chanting
- Doublespeak (confidently using words in a way that don't mean what they seem to, in order to prevent coherent thinking)
- Detailed control (of who you speak to, what you listen to, who you socialize with)
- Enemy creation ideology (us vs them) - in an atmosphere of fear (including the use of ridicule and the creation of a siege mentality)

Chapter 4 - Subliminal influencing: Persuasion You're Not Aware of

Information overload is becoming a global epidemic as we are constantly bombarded with various types of news each and every day. Being well-informed is important, but unfortunately much of the information that reaches us is either trivial or insignificant. However, that's not nearly as worrying as the kind of material we are absorbing daily. It is believed so-called 'Subliminal Influencing' is carried out on us by political parties, major corporations, marketing companies, governments, via social media apps and through pop videos among other things.

'Priming' is a well-known psychological effect which explains that by encountering a certain stimulus it will trigger related ideas in the mind. Because this one thing was activated, it influences other psychological processes related to it, which can go on to influence our desires or the choices we make.

This can work in either a positive or negative way. We can 'prime' ourselves for positive action by labeling our daily tasks in an extravagant and exciting way. Instead of simply 'exercising', you can tell yourself you will be spending an hour 'sculpting an amazing body'. Although the task is essentially the same, you have primed yourself to be more excited to do it by re-wording it into a more interesting and stimulating way. Priming can also be used in a negative context. You may be preparing for a regular meeting with your boss but prior to the meeting he sends you an e-mail titled URGENT and highlights within the e-mail that this will be an 'important' meeting. Now you have been primed to perhaps fear something you otherwise weren't too concerned about.

Psychological research has shown just how easily people are influenced by the world and people around them. We think we are this independent person who makes all their own choices themselves. When in actual fact we take unconscious direction our environment which is continuously controlling our sublte behaviors. One study discovered that if people can smell cleaning liquid 'in the air' they're more likely to tidy up. Or when people spotted a briefcase, they were likely to be competitive. We can even be influenced by simply catching a glimpse of certain words such as 'support' or 'helpful'; seeing these words makes us more likely to cooperate with others. These things occur without us ever realizing what's going on.

This is not deliberate mind control or manipulation but something that is quite natural. This shows how our unconscious buttons are pressed from everyday things.

Hidden Messages

Stressful jobs and long working hours mean that most people sprawl out on the couch in front of the TV or surf the Internet for many hours as soon as they get home. Both these pastimes help with relaxation; however, is believed that when the mind is relaxed, it is much more susceptible to subliminal persuasion and more likely to take in external messages subconsciously.

What happens while watching television (or anything else relaxing), is that brain waves transfer from a beta frequency (alert state of mind) to an alpha frequency (relaxed state of mind). When alpha waves predominate, the brain becomes highly receptive to suggestions. This is the state of mind which hypnotists try to put their subjects into before introducing persuasive suggestions.

Subliminal influencing is thought to be concealed within messages behind benign audio, images and video footage.

Such messages, are alleged to be camouflaged into the background of such stimulii and therefore not easily discernible. However, they influence us because, the subconscious mind is still able to detect them.

For many years people have feared that an image flashed on the screen which they didn't notice had the power to make them purchase a particular item. But is this even possible? You may wonder how long something has to be presented to us before we can detect it? This duration is said to be around 0.003 seconds, which is too quick for most of us to consciously pick up.

Some believe these hidden messages are controlling us by appealing to our unconscious desires. By supposedly influencing our perceptions through commercial advertising we are propelled into buying the latest new gadget or fashion accessory or having our voting decisions swayed via political propaganda. The understanding of such phenomena is that such messages are carefully manufactured to trigger people emotionally. Since humans are primarily feeling beings, appealing to their emotions (in theory) would make us more susceptible to influence.

Subliminal influence is similar to auto-suggestion or hypnosis wherein the subject is encouraged (or induced) to be relaxed so that suggestions can be directed to deeper parts of their mind where they can have the desired effect. Psychologists have even gone as far as to state that 'the unconscious mind is incapable of the critical refusal of hypnotic or subliminal suggestions'.

If this type of subliminal programming is, in fact, possible, then once an idea is planted into the subconscious, it would be very hard to get overide. Once it's stored there, the conscious thinking part of the mind doesn't have direct access to it. This is one of the reasons why some people nowadays avoid watching TV. Although most of us do so as it helps us relax, others believe we're being indoctrinated to act or live in a certain way and that a mass but delicate hypnosis is being conducted on the populations of the Earth.

The idea of subliminal advertising was introduced back in 1957, when a study was published by James Vicary and Frances Thayer who made the claim that when the words 'Drink Coca-Cola' and 'Eat popcorn' were subliminally presented to people watching a film, it increased sales of popcorn and coca cola by 18% and 58%, respectively. Once studies like this captured people's imagination they started to become worried they were being 'controlled' or influenced into buying certain products or voting for certain politicians. The fear was further compounded when people realized they were helpless against this sort of influencing and had no way of preventing it. Later on, it came out that Vicary and Thayer had manufactured the whole idea to promote their advertising and marketing agency. Later studies actually found that subliminal advertising wasn't as powerful as people had once anticipated. However, many remain convinced they're being influenced subliminally through television, radio, and advertising.

Since then, other studies have proven we're somewhat susceptible to subliminal influence. A later study showed that when words which related to being thirsty were subliminally presented to thirsty people, they actually drank more. Other studies supported this notion, such as customers were more likely to buy German wine from a store if German music was playing in the background and Italian wine if Italian music was playing. When the customers were asked afterward about their purchases they didn't even mention the music and were for the most part unaware of its influence.

So why was previous evidence shown to be unfounded yet other evidence proved that subliminal influencing does in fact work? There are two main factors to consider here. Firstly, for subliminal influence to have an impact, it must resonate with the current goals or needs of the individual. This is seen in the study of people who were subliminally influenced when they were thirsty, which led them to drink more. Secondly, any subliminal influence needs to be indirect and outside of our awareness to have an impact. For instance, the customers who heard the German or Italian music and then made purchases, as a result, weren't being directly influenced. But flashing the words 'drink Coca-Cola' or 'eat popcorn' are direct and it seems there are not as effective. It was later discovered that if the people buying the wine were made aware that their choices were influenced by the background music, they would have been more likely to purchase a different wine. It seems that even though we are susceptible to subliminal influence, we certainly don't like it. Another example showed that in restaurants where fast paced music was played, customers eat faster, and restaurants had a higher turnover rate of customers. The tempo of the music was influencing people to get moving.

We shouldn't be overly concerned about ads making us buy

things we don't want, or making us vote for political parties we hate. At the most, they can make us buy things we are already inclined to purchase or vote for a party we already had some interest in. It's unlikely we could ever be influenced into doing specific things against our will. Such ads can have an effect but not powerfully enough. But, we are susceptible to subliminal influence when it is presented in the right way and time. Next time you're out shopping pay attention to your immediate surroundings and notice if there's anything which might be influencing your buying decisions.

It is worth mentioning that subliminal influencing is not only about exploitation. People do use it for self-help purposes, to help them manage health, lose weight, stop smoking, improve self-esteem, develop good habits, overcome fears and the like.

Media Manipulation

Media is a very powerful tool for influencing mass thinking and can work in a number of ways depending upon what needs to be achieved. As discussed, it can't make us do specific things. But it does have the power to generally push us into a certain direction or way of thinking. Once whole populations are moving in the same direction, momentum is gained and reversing it can become very difficult. A person's identity can be profoundly influenced by a set of social influence techniques where a 'new identity' is purposefully created – which teaches us to be dependent on the leader or group ideology. The person, therefore, cannot think for him or herself but believes otherwise.

Big corporations and governments are believed to be amongst the biggest users of various sophisticated, technological and psychological methods of influencing our minds and psychology.

- Education

In many countries (in the East and West), education is used to ensure next generations will be obedient and controlled in order to fit into the current model of society. This is healthy to a certain degree, but some argue it is taken too far. Most education systems follow the same general principles: Individualism is discouraged over group thinking; the need for obedience and dependency is endorsed; only government-approved sources of information are used; propaganda is used extensively; alternative belief systems are painted negatively or disregarded; feelings such as homesickness, depression or resentment are blocked; students are encouraged to follow ideas that the government and society approves of such as committing to long-term education (i.e. university) – 'if they don't want to fail'.

- <u>Sports, politics, religion</u>

A system where the inherent tribal tendencies of humans are exploited by encouraging them to cooperate and unite by forming teams, so to direct their collective focus toward domination and winning.

- <u>TV and mass media</u>

TV and mass media enable some of the most successful methods of spreading (mis)information, promoting fear, impending chaos (our nation is under threat....), and using uncertainty to sell (who knows if you'll have a job next year, go on your dream vacation now....).

The majority of TV programs and media outlets (newspapers, magazines, news channels) are produced by a few mega-corporations which monitor what we watch, hear and read. Not only do they present the news they want us to hear, but they also distract people by preoccupying their minds with trivia like celebrity scandals and sports news.

These are just a few techniques used by the powerful to influence populations to move and think in the way they desire.

As the famous human rights activist Malcolm X once put it, 'The media's the most powerful entity on earth. They have the power to make the innocent guilty and to make the guilty innocent, and that's power. Because they control the minds of the masses'.

8 most common ways of media manipulation:

➢ *Distracting the public*

This technique relies on using nationalism or inspiring fear and hatred towards a foreign country or towards a particular group. Populations can be induced into fearful states by separating them into groups and making them appear different from other groups. The individuals then naturally look for any differences between themselves and the opposing group which works to separate them even further. This makes masses of people easier to control which helps serve the agenda of those trying to gain power. This tactic is usually deployed on the basis of religion, culture or race.

➤ *Distraction by major events*

Commonly known as a 'smokescreen', this technique consists of making the public focus its attention on something apparently interesting, but which serves to make sure we don't focus what is really important going on at that moment. Often times the propagandist doesn't want our focus on something which goes against their agenda.

➤ *Guilt by association*

When the media wants to destroy a person's character publicly they will somehow associate them to something the masses would be horrified with. Or, connect the individual to some law-breaking person, organization or action.

➤ *Just a little poison*

This implies slowly administering poison (lies) about someone, while at the same time writing about good things related to the same person. The human mind naturally tends to focus and remember the shocking and bad things. As the saying goes, 'it can take years to build a good reputation but only 5 minutes to ruin it'.

➤ *Make it funny*

If they can't destroy someone, the media may try to at least make people look ridiculous, by showing photos of someone's bad side, where they look stupid, ugly, wrinkled, overweight etc. The opposite is also true, if the media wants to support someone, they'll show photos where that person looks handsome, beautiful, photogenic and dignified.

➤ *Making sandwiches*

If they can't openly attack someone, the media publishes articles which are not entirely bad but which instead carry a bad tone. They may add some good (true) things about the person, but they make sure the article starts and closes with negativity and doubt. This is usually enough to make the public suspicious. We naturally focus more at the beginning and the end of any stimulus.

➤ *Stacking the experts*

This is a technique often used in TV panel debates. Participants are carefully chosen beforehand but in such a way that the obvious disbalance is made to look balanced. For example, they invite several members who have similar views, but just one member of an opposing viewpoint whom they would like to discredit. No matter how strong this participant is on their own, they stand little chance of winning such a debate.

➤ *Repetition makes true*

Incessant repetition of a lie eventually registers as truth in the mind of the masses. Mass hysteria can be created by repeatedly reporting the dangers of some microbe infesting humans which can take over the world which can leave populations in tones of panic.

As Joseph Goebbels, Adolf Hitler's propaganda minister said, 'If you repeat a lie often enough, it becomes the truth.'

Subliminal Persuasion Techniques

Subliminal persuasion is a way of getting others to agree with you without openly suggesting anything and without them ever noticing that you're trying to persuade them.

Good persuaders have a knack of communicating with a person's subconscious mind so they use a series of techniques without the other person ever realizing it.

> ➢ *Give them what they want*

Get people believing it was THEIR idea. Repeat what they're saying pretending you agree with the idea, and then about how you'll achieve what they want. People, like being right and feeling appreciated, so, will gladly go along with what you say you'll do, all the time pretending it was them who suggested it. For instance, you may want to go to a particular restaurant with a work colleague but it's their turn to decide where to eat. So, you may ask them what they feel like eating? Regardless of their response, a skilled manipulator will direct the questioning to take them to the outcome they desire.

➢ *Associate yourself with good things*

Make sure your clients (or whomever you're trying to persuade) feels good about meeting with you. Meet them in a pleasant environment. If possible, always negotiate over lunch in a nice restaurant and foot the bill. After a couple of pleasant experiences, they'll come to associate you with good things, while becoming agreeable and more open to meeting with you in future. We can take this tactic even further by engineering our social media feeds to promote certain ideals which the other party views as favorable. For example, a teenager trying to create attraction with his crush might post images of himself attending the concert of a band which his crush adores. Through this, she will associate her admirer with something she sees as good therefore viewing him in a more favorable light also.

➢ *Establish rapport*

Probably the most widely used yet simple persuasion techniques - Making others feel at ease in your presence. Rapport can be built by finding what you share in common with the person you're trying to influence. This is a tactic commonly used in consumer sales. Finding commonalities makes people feel 'we are similar to them', allowing them to naturally open up to us. Once someone lets their guard down, they become much easier to figure out.

Getting to know the person you're trying to influence will help them develop a degree of trust in you. By showing we trust them, they are more likely to reciprocate this by trusting us. However, be prepared to play various roles with the people you're interacting with. Sometimes you'll need to act like you're below them, sometimes their equal and sometimes an authority figure. Quickly acknowledging the other person's personality and character allows us to slip into one of these three roles more effectively.

Once you have chosen what position to take, pay closer attention and have a genuine interest in what they're saying or doing. Once we have a real interest in something, our entire body language changes. Your target will easily detect this and be much more receptive to your ideas, offers or suggestions. Subtle rapport building tricks include mirroring body language or matching the tone and speed of the other person's voice. Matching makes us appear more likable.

➢ *Use your words masterfully*

Developing good negotiation skills, in business or your private life, is something that can be learned. The first and most simple step is to use words in such a way that makes it easy for others to agree with what you want. For example, instead of asking, 'Would you be able to go on that trip?', say 'How soon can you go?'. This way of asking for someone's compliance implies the outcome has already been agreed. You're effectively not giving them the option to say No. This is also often used in sales negotiations, at the end of a sales pitch the salesperson may ask 'How would you like to pay?', without ever asking for consent if the customer was interested in the product.

➤ *Use a Persons' Name or Title repeatedly*

In the world-renowned book – How to win friends and influence people, the author Dale Carnegie discovered many factors in becoming more influential. One of the most popular is using someone's name or associated title. He believed that hearing your own name is one of the best and sweetest sounds for each of us. This may go back to our early childhood days when our name was repeated many times in loving tones. A person's name is essentially a core part of who they are, therefore hearing it validates our existence and makes us feel more positive about the person we heard it from. Taking this a step further we can apply titles to people if we want to influence them to behave how we would like, words such as 'mate', 'bro' or 'boss' can help control how other people treat us. Using such terms becomes a self-fulfilling prophecy. The person naturally acts more like what we refer to them as.

This is also seen in the development of young children, sometimes to devastating effect. If a child is constantly being told they're bad or worthless, they'll internalize this belief and grow up believing this to be true resulting in low self-worth.

➤ *The Power of Suggestion*

This technique is most effective when something unexpected has happened. Or when we feel the proverbial carpet has been pulled out from under our feet. When something happens that throws us off balance, we're much more likely to accept a suggestion that we would normally refuse.

If you choose such an unpredictable moment to suggest a 'solution' to someone's problem, but in fact, you're asking them to do what's in your interests. The other party is much more likely to accept your proposal then they would under normal circumstances. This is because people are more receptive to new ideas when they're disorientated or unsettled.

The mind has to work harder to process new or different experiences, which leads to the lowering of other mental functions (such as decision making) for a short period of time. As a countermeasure, never sign or agree to something when you don't feel fully 'centered' because you are much more vulnerable to manipulation in this state.

Chapter 5 - Brainwashing

Brainwashing is one of the more aggressive forms of manipulation. It is more commonly used by cults, religious or political leaders, with prisoners of war and in abusive relationships.

Being brainwashed creates confusion about your identity. Feelings of self-doubt are the first signs of being brainwashed, even though we're not always aware of what's happening.

Personality traits such as self-doubt, a weak sense of self, lacking confidence or feeling guilty are enough to make one susceptible to brainwashing. The opposite is also true, a stronger sense of self and emotional stability makes us more resistant to such techniques. So not everyone is a good candidate for brainwashing. Certain techniques which are taught to soldiers can help prevent them from being brainwashed. These include using visualizations, repetition of mantras and other related meditation methods. Also having knowledge as to exactly how brainwashing works (Lifton's theory described later in this chapter) helps strengthen the psyche against such an attack.

It's not only others who brainwash us, we sometimes do it to ourselves by blindly accepting everything we hear and read. If for instance, you start associating with negative people or living in an environment which instills feelings of fear or self-doubt, you may undergo a subtle change in personality and character. On the flip-side people suffering from low self-esteem or confidence, can 'brainwash' themselves through affirmations, meditations, reading and learning how to become the people they would most like to be – confident, charming, successful or whatever. Through constant reinforcement and repetition of either positive or negative stimulus, we change as a result.

It is often said in self-help circles that the people we surround ourselves with mirror back to us who we are likely to become in the future. Surround yourself with happy, successful people and you'll be more likely to become happy and successful. Surround yourself with negative people and you will also become more like them.

Signs you're being brainwashed

Signs of being brainwashed vary from intense and dangerous brainwashing by cult leaders or psychopaths to everyday subliminal influencing we endure from our families, employers, the Government, commercials, culture and social media.

If we're constantly fed similar information through repetition, day after day, month after month and year after year, you eventually start becoming it, no matter how ludicrous it might be. Brainwashing happens every day to young children. How children are programmed from a young age is effectively brainwashing. When the personality has not yet fully formed it is highly impressionable.

If you were fortunate enough to have been brought up by a loving, positive and supportive family, you will have probably developed adequate defense mechanisms by the time you reach adolescence. However, if your parenting was not predominantly positive, it likely filled your mind with negative and self-limiting beliefs.

Character-development can be a long difficult process and without sufficient self-esteem instilled in the earlier part of life, we're unlikely to develop the confidence we will need later in life. But it's hard to develop self-esteem if we're repeatedly told whilst growing up, 'I don't think you'll ever amount to much', or 'You're good for nothing', or 'I don't think you have it in you to succeed', such statements may not have been passed with much conviction, but they tend to stay with us and color how we perceive the world and ourselves. Although parents usually mean well, they sometimes do damage, especially if they believe they're encouraging us to work harder by hinting that we're stupid, or that everybody else is smarter or better behaved. All though reverse psychology can work, its usually not helpful for young developing minds.

Our culture brainwashes us into believing that we are not pretty enough, smart enough or good enough for what we want in life. After years of being told such things, we start unconsciously believing them, even though our ego may reject the suggestion as unfair or wrong, these limiting beliefs run in the background of our programming.

Many of us go through life afraid of going for what our heart desires because from a young age we have been brainwashed into believing we're not good enough or deserving of what we truly want.

Systematic Breakdown of Brainwashing

In psychological domains, brainwashing is known as 'thought reforming', which is closely related to social influence, in which we are being influenced by society and our environment constantly.

Brainwashing is comprised of 3 different methods of mind control which is why it's so effective. Firstly, it involves the 'compliance' technique, this looks to change someone's behavior but is not concerned with the subject's current beliefs, it's the 'just do it' attitude. The second method used is Persuasion, 'do it because you'll gain something - feel happier, more positive, healthy, successful'. The third and final method is education, this is also known as the 'propaganda method' - where we are taught things we don't necessarily believe in. This method is also the most like brainwashing as it tries to change a person's understanding and beliefs. The underlying rule here is, 'do it because it's the right thing to do'.

Brainwashing is comprised of these three aspects, which when used coherently makes it a powerful form of influence that eventually overrides a person's will.

Since brainwashing is such an extreme form of mind control, it requires certain pre-requisites for it to be successful. Some of the key elements needed include complete isolation and absolute dependency from the subject, this is why it tends to happen more in isolated situations such as prisons and cults for example. For brainwashing to be successful the manipulator must have complete control over the victim. This includes controlling their sleep patterns, meal times, use of bathroom and any other fulfillment of basic human needs. Through such a heavy dependency, the target's identity eventually breaks, to the point they don't know who they are anymore. At this moment, they can be 'brainwashed' with a new set of ideas, beliefs, attitudes, and behaviors.

So, brainwashing is possible under the specific conditions mentioned, but at the same time, it's difficult for this to occur in everyday life. Also, the effects of brainwashing are usually not long-term because the victim's true self and original identity can never be completely erased but can be hidden or repressed for a short amount of time. Once the 'new identity' stops being enforced the victim's original thoughts and beliefs gradually begin to resurface.

In the 1950's, an American psychologist Robert Jay Lifton studied the effects the Korean war and Chinese camps had on its prisoners. A number of American soldiers had been captured during the Korean way and brainwashed. He uncovered the specific steps which were undertaken to break the prisoners down and open them up to be brainwashed. These processes began by breaking down the prisoners 'sense of self' which would eventually lead to a change in attitude and beliefs. Using Lifton's school of thought, we can break down brainwashing into main three sections.

1. Breaking down of the original self
2. Introducing a possibility of Salvation
3. Rebuilding the Self

With the basic structure in place. Lifton further broke down the brainwashing process into 10 individual stages (A-J) -

A. Assault on Identity

B. Guilt

C. Self-Betrayal

D. Breaking Point

E. Leniency

F. Compulsion to confess

G. Channeling of guilt
H. Releasing guilt
I. Progress and Harmony
J. Final Confession & Rebirth

Every one of these stages is carried out in complete isolation, which means normal social and environmental reference points are absent. These initial influencers are enhanced by 'mind-clouding' methods such as hunger and sleep deprivation - both of which make the target considerably weaker. This is further compounded by a constant threat of violence or harm. All these factors prevent the victim from being able to think independently and critically.

1. Breaking down of the original self

This comprises of sections A-D of the ten stages of brainwashing.

A. Assault on Identity

The brainwashing process begins with attacks on the target's sense of self (ego/identity) – When we're not being ourselves, our core belief system is disrupted. The brainwasher will deny the victim of everything he thinks he is i.e. 'you're not a soldier', 'you're not American' etc. This can continue for weeks or even months, to the point the target is left incredibly disorientated, confused and fatigued. Gradually, his beliefs about himself begin to weaken.

B. Guilt

As the identity crisis is beginning to take root, the target is made to feel a crushing sense of guilt that he is bad. He is continuously targeted for any minor things and attacked for the sins he has committed. This can include everything from his beliefs about himself to the way he eats or drinks. By increasing the feelings of guilt and shame, he feels that everything he does is wrong or bad.

C. Self-Betrayal

As the victim is wallowing in self-guilt and shame, he is forced or threatened into dis-identifying from his family, friends, country, peers or anyone who holds the same 'bad' belief systems as him. Such a betrayal of his own values and of those he feels some loyalty towards increases the feelings of shame while further losing touch with his identity.

D. Breaking Point

At this stage, the target is 'broken' and begins to question himself. He doesn't know who he is anymore and asks, 'Who am I and what am I supposed to do?' With the impact of the identity breakdown, feelings of deep shame and unworthiness increase. Along with betraying his long-standing beliefs, the victim goes through a 'nervous breakdown' - which includes depression, emotional suffering, and disorientation. The target at this point will feel completely alone and be incredibly vulnerable as he's lost all understanding of himself. Here the manipulator introduces a new belief system as a reprise to prevent the suffering.

2. Introducing possibility of Salvation

The brainwashing process now moves into the second of the three stages.

E. Leniency

The victim is offered help and support. With the target in such a compromised state, they are presented with a small act of kindness or relief from the constant abuse. This may be in the shape of food or via an emotional connection. For instance, the manipulator may ask the victim personal questions about his life and interests. In the wake of long psychological suffering, any small act of kindness can seem huge. This makes the victim feel a sense of gratitude and relief which is disproportionate to the offering, he may almost feel like he's been 'saved'.

F. Compulsion to confess

For the first time, the target feels a sense of relief from the constant assault on him and his character. In response to this, he feels compelled to reciprocate the acts of kindness he has received by possibly confessing his part in the war. This will help him to feel further relief from the guilt and shame which he has been feeling.

G. Channeling of guilt

After prolonged periods of pain, confusion, breakdowns with brief moments of reprieve the victim's sense of guilt has lost meaning. He now doesn't know what he has done wrong, he just feels himself to be wrong. This makes the target a clean slate, which opens the door for the manipulator to begin influencing him. He can 'channel' the victim's guilt into any areas or subjects as he decides. He will relate the victim's guilt to his beliefs, such as the country he serves, which is why he feels bad. The contrast between the old painful beliefs and new (relieving) beliefs is established. The old is linked to pain and psychological disturbance whereas the new is associated with the possibility of relief and no pain. This is an NLP technique which helps create new 'neuro-associations' within the mind.

H. Releasing guilt

The victim comes to understand that it's not himself who is guilty or shameful but in fact his beliefs. These are the cause of the bad painful feelings he feels. So, he begins to believe he can escape the pain by dis-identifying from the old beliefs. All it requires is that he denounces everything he thought he was associated with (his old belief system) and the pain will be relieved. At this point, the victim will confess even more. With these confessions, he is also releasing the old belief system and as a result, is pushing his old identity further away.

3. Rebuilding the Self

I. Progress and Harmony

The victim feels he now has a choice. He is introduced to a new way of thinking, which is shown as the 'right' way. At this point, the abuse has come to a halt. Instead, the target is offered comfort and suffers less psychological disturbances, which makes him neurologically associate the relief with the new 'good' belief system. Like classic manipulation tactics, the victim feels like he has the freedom of choice to decide between the old set of beliefs or the new ones presented to him. Since the target has already dis-identified from his old beliefs in response to leniency, by making his choice to choose the 'new' belief system he releases his feelings of guilt further. His new identity and sense of self-feels safer since it's nothing like the old one which led to his breakdown.

J. Final Confession & Rebirth

At the final stage, the victim is 'converted' and feels a sense of rebirth. He may declare he has chosen 'good' over evil. With the contrasting difference of the painful old ways, with the relief of the new, he hangs to his new identity as though it saved his life. He rejects his old belief system and even turns against it. To close the process there maybe rituals and ceremonies carried out by the manipulators to welcome the target into his new community.

This detailed description of the brainwashing process was created by Lifton after his study of war prisoners from the Korean War.

Brainwashing Techniques

As we now understand, brainwashing doesn't occur overnight but is usually a series of actions taken simultaneously over a period of time, which eventually results into a changed personality. Perception and behavior change, sometimes to such an extent that the victim becomes unrecognizable to their friends or peers.

The techniques used and the speed with which the personality changes depends on many things, but most of all on whether the target is being subjected to brainwashing against their will (in which case they'll naturally resist as much as they can) or whether they don't know they're being brainwashed (e.g. in cults) and believe all the ideas being impressed upon them are their own and that they themselves are making the decisions. This could be deemed successful brainwashing, as the victim is unaware of what's occurring.

Most common overt and covert brainwashing techniques:

➤ *Repetition and nagging*

It's hard not to start believing something or at least begin doubting one's self if someone is constantly repeating the same thing over and over every day, for months or even years.

➤ *Isolation*

It is easier to control someone if they have no access to sources of information which conflict with the brainwashing material. If the target talks to someone about the ideas being imposed upon them and other people understand what's happening, they may scupper the chances for a successful brainwash. This tactic is often witnessed in abusive relationships, where one partner doesn't want the other to communicate with friends or family incase their motives are uncovered.

➤ Blind obedience

This prevents the victim from thinking for themselves.

➤ Responsibility

One central brainwashing technique is to make someone feel responsible for their faults and the things that go wrong in their life. If they make mistakes, do something poorly, or if things don't go according to plan, making them feel responsible leaves them feeling negative emotions such as guilt and shame, which lowers their defenses and opens them up for manipulation.

➤ Guilt and fear

These are used extensively as part of an overall emotional manipulation plan. When a huge guilt complex is imposed, we start believing we're deserving of any resulting punishment.

➤ Love bombing

Some cults shower new members with love and attention to make them feel special and part of their 'family'. These childish games cause age regression and encourage obedience.

> ***My way is the right way attitude***

No questions or criticism of leadership is allowed. When everyone is obedient, the group is easier to control - Group think.

> ***Repetitive, mind-dumbing practices***

Chanting, singing, dancing and body therapies all reduce critical thinking. Research shows our brain can only focus on one thing at a time, so a great way to slow down the thinking process (which may lead to questioning) is by engaging in repetitive chants or similar activities.

The aim of these techniques is to prompt the target into accepting new ideas blindly, without questioning. For that to happen, the mind has to become dormant – hypnotized, drugged or made helpless, powerless or childlike.

As Mokokoma Mokhonoana once said, 'Most people do not have a problem with you thinking for yourself, as long as your conclusions are the same as or at least compatible with their beliefs.'

Brainwashing yourself into positive thinking

Although brainwashing is deemed a negative practice and is generally associated with mental abuse it can also be used for positive purposes by helping us overcome bad habits, insecurities or low self-esteem and confidence. By simply applying various brainwashing techniques we can positively impact our psychology.

Self-brainwashing can be used as a form of self-help therapy of replacing old, outdated thought patterns with new healthier programs which can help us get more out of life.

The key word here is BELIEF. Just as the famous Law of Attraction states - you get what you think you'll get! With self-brainwashing, if you convince yourself you can do something, you'll eventually develop the courage to do so. But if you believe you can't, you will likely be right also.

4 Self-brainwashing techniques:

− *Identify a negative thought pattern*

Identify a negative thought or belief that's been holding you back. How long have you felt this way? Can you connect the programming to any early life experiences? Are you aware of how this belief has affected your life? What do you think your life would have been like if it weren't for this negative thought pattern? Do you believe you are what others tell you? What skills or abilities do you wish you had?

− *Acknowledging the damage*

Be aware of any negative emotional, mental or physical harm this thought pattern has done to you, then make the decision to do something about it. Negative programming can be reversed, but it takes time, so be prepared to work on this issue for a long time if need be.

− *The Power of Suggestion*

Much of our negative thinking comes from suggestions we take in from others. Think of how many times someone has spoken to you negatively, said you were fat, stupid or unintelligent? Eventually, when these suggestions are heard repeatedly they tend to became our reality.

We can reverse such damage by purposefully taking our suggestions onto a more positive path by consciously choosing positive beliefs. Whatever flaws you believe you have, they can often be reversed. One such way is to constantly tell yourself what you'd like to become, by verbally affirming (or thinking) how successful, healthy or confident you are. Eventually, with commitment, these suggestions can come true as our actions and behaviors gradually begin to follow the constant positive reinforcement we're feeding ourselves.

− *Repetition*

Repetition is successfully used in self-brainwashing. Consistently reinforce positive thoughts about yourself or your self-image by repeating confidence-boosting words and affirmations throughout the day. If it helps, use sticky notes on your desk, inside your car, on the fridge, and other places where you'll often see them. Or, try chanting short phrases such as, 'I am smart', 'I am successful', 'People like me' or whatever you're trying to change.

Alternatively, you can make it a daily habit to rewrite your chosen affirmations over and over in a notebook or journal. Constantly seeing and hearing the same ideas eventually results in constant belief in them as they are accepted and integrated by the subconscious.

We can take this further by reading books associated with the skills we want to develop, listening to audiobooks or watching Youtube videos about the related topic. With a constant bombardment from various modalities, we begin to influence and change our psychology.

Chapter 6 - The Most Powerful Mind-Power Tool

Neuro-Linguistic Programming (NLP) is a model based on human performance derived from studying people who have achieved outstanding results in life. If we deconstruct the term Neuro-Linguistic, we see on closer inspection that it involves using language (linguistic) to reprogram the brain/mind (neuro).

Language in this sense doesn't only involve the words we speak. Through NLP we can understand how people organize their feelings, thoughts, words, behaviors and emotions to achieve the results they most desire. By simply following the mental blueprint of other successful people, we too can change our behavior to produce similar results. According to NLP practitioners, individual success has a lot to do with developing good communication skills. NLP is something anyone can learn to improve their effectiveness, both personally and professionally. These techniques are simple to apply to any area of life and are most commonly used for building positive habits and rituals.

NLP was developed by Richard Bandler after observing that some people excelled in certain areas of life while others either struggled, gave up or failed. Research carried out revolved around the question of - *How was it that some get outstanding results, while others, equally educated or experienced, don't?* What the study found was that there was an underlying pattern of thoughts and communication (internal dialogue) that helped some people achieve the desired results.

NLP therefore outlines the specific processes of how the personality creates and manifests itself. How the perceptions we develop as children, gradually turn into our beliefs and expectations. How our mind filters, distorts and magnifies information we pick up from our environment and then processes it in order to successfully match it to our internal programs. This is how we have evolved and how we make sense of life - internal programming combined with external stimuli.

NLP Techniques for Manipulation

Although NLP clearly has many positive uses it can also be used in influencing others. Magicians often trick their audiences using an advanced array of these methods. NLP will teach you how to bypass the conscious, analytical mind (mental short-cutting) while engaging the unconscious - the more receptive part of the mind. Non-verbal communication is a subtle but very powerful way of achieving this.

The keys to applying NLP techniques successfully for manipulation purposes is by adhering to these basic principles:

- Be clear about what you want to achieve.
- Establish rapport with the person you are attempting to influence to understand their perspective.
- Be aware of any subtle signs the opposite party is portraying.
- Be flexible.

➤ *Vague Language*

The main purpose of vague language is to induce a hypnotic trance. Various studies have found that the less we understand something, the more we are led into unconscious trance states because we're less liable to disagree or react. Alternatively, the more specific and understandable something is, the more alert and aware we become.

Vague words are easier for people to say yes to. It's easier to get people to agree to improving "education", having "excitement", achieving "success", or developing "motivation".

➢ *Anchoring*

Anchoring is a technique used to induce a certain frame of mind or emotion, such as happiness or relaxation. It usually involves a touch, gesture or a word which serves as the 'anchor'.

Anchoring is really quite simple - start by recalling a happy memory. Feel it. See it clearly in your mind's eye. Get in touch with all the positive emotions and feelings related to this moment. Next, hold your thumb and middle finger together on either hand, gently give your fingers two quick squeezes. Repeat this process several times while thinking about your happy moment, each time make the feelings of happiness or confidence stronger. This is called "laying the anchor". Later, whenever you require this feel-good emotion, you can recall the anchor by using the same double-squeeze method to recall the sense of happiness you felt when remembering your happy moment. You have essentially programmed yourself to identify squeezing your fingers together as something which feels good.

You can also use this technique to anchor others and influence their mind state. For example, if the person you're trying to influence happens to be in a heightened emotional state, such as happy, sad or angry – touch them while they are in this state, i.e. tap them on the shoulder or placing your hand on their arm etc. If you manage to do this on several occasions while they're experiencing this heightened emotional state, you will have "anchored" them. So, whenever you need to get them into similar state, happy, sad or angry, all you'll have to do is touch them in the same way as you did originally. Their brain will associate your touch with the feelings they were experiencing when you anchored them. Voila!

Mental Short-cuts

Now we will consider how 'mental shortcuts' can be used to manipulate and influence.

We all use mental shortcuts to get us through our lives. These programming's occur automatically without much deliberate thought. Due to the complexity of the world we live in, there is no way we could consciously keep track of every little thing that is happening around us. Take, for example, driving a car. If you go back to the time when you were first learning to drive, your attention was on many things. But over time and with constant repetition you learned to just do it, without much thought. But how? The answer is by using shortcuts. So instead of noticing every little thing such as, looking around, accelerating, braking, using mirrors, indicators and then carefully driving. Overtime you created a psychological shortcut, where you internalized each of these individual components into your mind and nervous system. All of these little tasks became one task – Driving. Now simply starting your car propels you into action and everything happens almost automatically.

We aren't consciously aware of when we're using shortcuts, we just do it. Since there is little thinking involved it may seem like it makes us vulnerable. As we blindly take action in response to some stimulus. But, we do need these shortcuts because without them we wouldn't get half as much done in life. We would be exhausted from having to think about every little task. Instead, we can make fast decisions with little effort and apply our focus where it is most needed.

All though NLP wasn't specifically designed for deceit. With such a tool, we can use behavioral shortcuts to manipulate and influence others.

Go for a Walk

Want to change someone's mind? Simple, go for a walk together.

This is an incredibly simple approach to influencing someone. It has been suggested within NLP teachings, that when we walk with someone we connect with them in a different way. The reason for this is incredibly simple. When we walk together we have to be in synch with one another, so we stay at a similar pace. This unified rhythm then influences our breathing and thoughts also. As we begin to connect in more ways, this allows the conversation to flow more easily also. This can help us move our ideas forward and get of what we want from our communications with others.

However, if you were having a discussion with someone whilst walking and you wanted to disagree with them, you would have to stop walking! This would give your argument much more impact. People in disagreement will rarely be seen walking together.

Learn to use this subtle tactic to your advantage. Next time you're in disagreement or at loggerheads with someone, suggest going for a stroll to iron out your differences.

Solving Your Problems with Chairs

Begin by sitting in a chair. Think about a problem you're struggling with or a decision you're stuck on. Put all your concentration, focus and emotions onto this issue. While doing this pay attention to your external surroundings. What do you notice about the room - lights, sounds, smells etc? Next, direct your attention inwards, how does your body feel when thinking about this issue?

Write down your observations.

Now, move chairs. Maybe sit in an opposite chair to the one you were seated in. But this time think about a situation which is the exact opposite of the original thought. Perhaps something more positive. Do not take too long trying to think of something, go with the first thing that comes to mind. Completely immerse yourself into this memory and pay attention to your inner and outer observations like you did the first time. Recreate the opposite vision in your mind and record all the feelings and sensations involved, including your posture, body language, tonality etc.

Finally, move back to the first seat you were in while keeping the second experience fresh in your mind and read the notes you had made about the second experience. Embody the feelings in your posture, emotions, and mind. You should now come to the perfect solution to your original problem. If this doesn't work the first time, continue to swap chairs. Even if you don't come up with an ideal solution you'll begin applying your second mental state (positive) to the problem. Making it appear less troublesome.

Mirroring and Matching

This is a well-known means of influencing someone's behavior. It simply involves mirroring the verbal and non-verbal behavior of the other person. We are naturally more open to influence by those we relate to. Put this into practice by matching someone's speaking style, their tonality, and language. If they're relaxed, be relaxed. If they're being more formal, do the same. Try to pay attention to their breathing pattern. Do they breathe deeply? Or shallow? Copy their breathing pattern also. Look them square in the eyes while occasionally repeating back to them what they have just said. This technique is even more powerful if it can be done with matching body language.

Another subtler tactic is once you're mirroring them, subliminally transmit messages to them. Think about emitting the perspective or state of mind you want to create in them.

Change Seats

If you find yourself in an argument or disagreement, try switching seats with the other person, this will allow you both to see things from each other's point of view. The sheer simplicity of this techniques can make it sound outrageous but give it a try, you'll be surprised by how changing your physical position can impact your mentality.

However, if you don't want to change your mindset but just want to influence the other. Try getting the other person to sit in your seat while you perhaps choose to stand and communicate. This will help signify the illusion of authority. By standing you'll appear bigger and more commanding.

All of these techniques, are allowing us to take advantage of psychological shortcuts.

Chapter 7 – Mind Control Techniques and Your Career

Most of us are aware of the term 'office politics' - this is something which happens in the place of work, where employees try to gain some advantage at the expense of their colleagues. Any such strategies tend to impact the working environment and working relationships. On the other hand, there is also the idea of good office politics which helps us to promote ourselves respectfully without offending others. This is often referred to as 'Networking'.

Many of us see office politics as something negative and to be avoided. But we can leverage office politics to help us become more proficient at work while contributing to our success. But by refusing to deal with or acknowledge the obvious politicking going on, you put yourself into a position where others can take an unfair advantage. If you can learn to play this game the right way, you can further your career and even those of your colleagues (if you so wish).

No escaping Office Politics

Here are some reasons why office politics are inevitable.

- Hierarchy of power. In most offices people are structed in a power based hierarchy. The most powerful at the top with the least influential at the bottom. This makes the people at the bottom naturally want to rise higher.

- Promotions & Career advancement - Many people desire to move up in their place of employment through gaining promotions. This can create competition between them and their colleagues while also causing disruption between teams and departments.

- Employees may try to influence decision makers by becoming overly friendly with them.

We can learn to use office politics in a positive way to help influence our position. The first step is to become a good observer, then use the information gained to develop a stronger network in which to operate in.

Re-organize Office Hierarchy

Office politics usually overrides the formal organizational structures. To find out who is really in charge, sit back and watch the dynamics at play within your organization. Re-structure the power chart in terms of who exercises the most power. Answer these questions to help determine the real movers and shakers.

- Who are the big influencers?
- Who has authority but doesn't enforce it?
- Who is the most respected?
- Who is the most feared?
- Who's the most helpful or mentor's others?
- Who is the real brains behind the operation? Without them everything would come to a halt?

From answering these questions, you should come to an understanding of how the power is really distributed.

Social Networks

Once you determine who plays what role in your company you have idea of where the power lies. The next step is to recognize the social networks to understand the power dynamics further. Look to find the answers to these questions.

- Who gets on with who?
- Are there groups or cliques within the organization?
- Is there anyone in conflict with another?
- Who struggles getting on with others?
- What are most relationships based upon? Friendship? Manipulation? Respect?
- How does the influence sway between different groups?

Developing Relationships

From the answers to these questions you should have developed a clear understanding of how the relationships within your company currently influence the organization. Now you can position yourself to build your own social network. Follow these guidelines to position yourself in a way that will help you move forward.

- Get to know the powerful people and the influencers. Don't be intimidated. If you've have been watching them closely, you'll know more about them than you realize.
- Develop relationships at all levels of the hierarchy. That

includes directors, managers, bosses, peers and even the caretaker. Include those who are above and below you. Some people tend to look down on those who have less power than them. This is ill advised. Never get too big for your boots!

- Build relationships with those who have social or informal power and influence.
- Build relationships based on trust, integrity and respect. Avoid needless flattery.
- Don't align yourself with one particular group. Be open and friendly with all influencers.
- Become part of various networks. That way you'll always be one step ahead.

Leverage your networks

If you have managed to make yourself a part of the most powerful and influential networks in your organization, you can leverage these relationships to promote yourself. Use your position within these groups to -

- Gain information which will help you
- Promote your successes and achievements
- Attract more opportunities
- Find ways to make yourself appear better

Once you have mapped the influential figures and groups in your organization you'll also have identified the people you would probably rather stay away from. But we recommend doing the opposite. As the saying goes, 'keep your friends close and your enemies closer'. Often the people we want to stay away from hold a certain degree of influence and keeping them on side can just help us stay clear of any animosity.

- Get to know these people. Be nice, pleasant and courteous to them.
- Do not share too much information with them.
- Try to understand what their goals are.
- Avoid any of their negative influence. These people generally need to use negative office politicking as a means of getting their needs met i.e. gossiping, a** kissing etc.

Regulate your own behavior and actions

Through these new learnings you should have a good understanding of what works in your organization and what doesn't. Watch and stay close to the successful people. Copy their behaviors. Do what they do. Here are some general pointers which will help you keep your head down but also keep you moving in the right direction.

- If you hear something interesting, keep hold of it. You might be able to use it as leverage at a later time.
- Avoid arguments and conflicts. If any disagreements occur, rise above and even apologize if you have too. Stay off the radar.
- Be assertive, not aggressive.
- Be careful with the information you share. Expect everything you say, to be disclosed to others.
- When voicing opinions or criticisms, keep in mind the power structure and if you're stepping on anyone's toes

Office politics are something that goes on around the entire world. By learning to use them in the right way, you'll look much competent compared to those who abuse it.

Here are some manipulative methods used every day in the work place. It's worth being aware of what these are, either to avoid being manipulated or to use these techniques for your own gain.

Controlled approval

The purpose of this technique is to create confusion while increasing the vulnerability of employees. Here the employer behaves inconsistently in his reactions to an employees' performances.

Alternating reward and punishment for the same actions, creates confusion. For instance, if you're in a managerial position, on one occasion praise someone for being assertive in a meeting then the next time disapprove of their assertiveness.

While this would make some employees give up trying to get things right (because you never know how the boss is going to react, so why bother?), but some will try even harder to please. It is the latter group of employees that are more desirable to the employer, as they're more submissive and obedient, therefore easier to manage. Passive people are easily kept on alert, they're anxious and desperate to get things right, which makes the manager's job easier.

Planting Ideas
While some things are best addressed directly and openly, there are also subtle but powerful ways of getting someone to do or believe something.

A manipulative way of influencing somebody's behavior or thoughts is to indirectly suggest certain things. This should be done in such a way that will either make them feel it was their idea in the first place or leave them with no option but to do what you've ask.

For example, if your plan is to save money by discouraging staff from having a Christmas party at an expensive venue. A month or so before the party, start mentioning that you may be able to consider a salary increase from January if the office running costs are cut by up to 30%. Mention this several times to the most influential staff members. Then a couple of weeks before Christmas leave several catering leaflets lying around the office, making sure your employee's see them.

Or, let's say, you work within an I.T department of a business and you want to recommend the purchase of new computers so mention something "in confidence" to someone you know is a gossip. You tell them how the old computers emanate more EMR (radiation) and start leaving leaflets on the dangers of EMR around the office, until someone from the staff asks management if the old IT equipment could be replaced anytime soon. You agree, and the staff appreciate your concern for their health, while management submit an order for new IT equipment from the IT provider you have a deal with. Bingo!

Labels

Labelling people as either good or bad can influence their behavior and performance. Calling someone smart, intelligent or competent can massively improve their performance as they'll want to live up to this positive label, which then becomes a self-fulfilling prophecy. For each person in your organization, understand how you want them to act towards you, then use this technique to condition them into behaving as that person. Calling someone 'mate' or 'buddy', will make them act friendlier or referring to someone as 'boss' will give them a heightened sense of importance.

Once we assign a 'label' to someone, we can then ask for requests which are consistent with the label we have given to them which will also be more likely to be fulfilled. For instance, calling someone a hard worker and then asking them to work overtime. The individual will find it difficult to say no as they want to live up to this positive image you've created.

Companies will also label consumers as a particular type of person in order to sell their product. Gillette's motto for example, 'the best a man can get' - implies men who buy their products are the best men.

Positive Reinforcement

This means thanking people for doing something the way you wanted it done. Everyone likes being appreciated and knowing that their hard work is noticed and rewarded. Such a simple gesture influences people to genuinely want to please you even more in future.

Hopefully this information can help you traverse the potential mine-field of your work place. We're all forced into developing relationships at work with people we may otherwise avoid. But learning to use these strategies to our advantage can help us get a step ahead.

Persuasion Slide

The Persuasion Slide was created by a blogger named Roger Dooley of Neuromarketing. He created this idea of using a slide to represent how various factors influence a consumer into making a decision in the business world.

The Persuasion Slide™

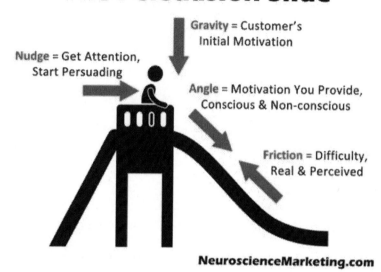

1. In the first step the customer is given a 'nudge' via social media, an advertisement, a friend, or some marketing kind of campaign.

2. The next stage is 'Gravity'- The customers inner motivations and desires provide the momentum to move them down the slide.

3. The angle is the next component - The slide has to be the correct angle, so the customer will go along all the way to the bottom and complete the sales process. If the customer has low internal motivation, then the angle of the slide would be steeper making it more difficult to reach the bottom smoothly. However, if extra motivation is added the angle will open up and allow an easier ride to the bottom. Extra motivation could

come in the form of better features and benefits then what the customer is currently experiencing. The angle here is critical - without the correct angle, slides don't work!!

4. The final part is 'Friction' - This is seen as any difficulties which may be encountered in completing the desired process, i.e. or converting the customer into a sale. Friction on a slide is seen in the child who gets stuck half way down. Friction is anything which works against us.

To outline the whole process again, the nudge at the beginning can come from anything persuasive such as the psychological theories described above. For instance, 'Amplification' can represent that the customer is reinforcing their values or attitudes as they propel downwards. Next social proof acts as a stronger push keeping them going all the way along and resulting in a quicker sale/conversion.

This example was used to explain how a customer can be persuaded in purchasing goods or a particular item. But I believe a similar system can be translated and applied to our personal interactions and dealings with others in day to day life.

10 Persuasion Theories in the Workplace

Here are some of the most popular persuasion techniques and theories you may be familiar with. Either because you've used them yourself or have had them used on you.

1. Amplification

When we express ourselves with positivity and passion that belief reinforces itself within us. So, we start to believe what we said, even more. This also has a powerful impact on influencing the opposite party. But the reverse is also true, if we express ourselves with a degree of uncertainty this softens our impact. Whatever we truly feel is amplified.

2. Conversion Theory

This theory suggests that a confident minority voice can be more influential than a majority. The minority can have a larger impact than their numbers would suggest. Those susceptible to influence in the majority are likely there because it was the popular choice and therefore easier for them to join. Humans are naturally social with tribal tendencies and feel safer within larger groups. Unfortunately, this need to belong can sometimes overrides our true beliefs and intentions.

3. Manipulation of Information

Conversations are made of up four main elements. We can deliberately break one of these four rules to persuade or manipulate. These four factors are -

Quantity - All information should be communicated in full. This means no intentional holding back of certain information.

Quality - Information should be honest and truthful. Again, this is something which can be manipulated to suit one's own personal needs or agenda.

Relative - The information given should relate to the matter/subject at hand. Sometimes a manipulator may give information outside of this criteria in a bid to distract.

Manner - Information should be expressed and communicated in a non-judgmental and easy to understand way.

We can usually tell when someone is being insincere based upon these factors. All these points are also expressed through non-verbal communication, tonality and body language.

4. Priming

Certain stimuli can affect how we think about and perceive things. For instance, a magician may use the word 'try' in one sentence, then 'cycle' in the next. With the intention of getting you to think about a 'tri-cycle'.

5. Reciprocity

This is a common behavior, where we return favors to others based upon what they have done for us. It's a technique which can be used intentionally to get desired results.

6. Scarcity factor

Humans are programmed to naturally want what is in short supply and tend to fear loss over gaining value. Desire is increased by the anticipation of regret if we miss out. These factors motivate us into taking faster action. Advertising campaigns sometimes play on this psychological loop hole to sell their products. For example, offering 70% off everything for a day, is usually enough to draw the punters in.

This method is about 1) tapping into the pain the target wants to avoid (regret) and 2) showing them how they can avoid it. Which can make you appear as though you've saved the day.

7. Sleeper impact

The same persuasive messages lose their impact on us over time. But messages coming from lower credibility sources seem to influence us more over the longer term. Say a sleazy car salesman tells you what's the best car for you to purchase, however you initially dismiss this advice because of the unreliable source. But overtime you begin to distance the source of the material (the salesman) from the information. As a result, you may find yourself looking for the vehicle he recommended.

8. Social

This has a huge impact on us. How well we relate to someone, influences how strongly we are persuaded by them. For instance, a close friend can get us to do something we wouldn't even consider if it came from someone we didn't know as well. In the same way, we are more trusting of big brands and popular sources as we gain social proof by relating to them.

9. Change approach

Yale University carried out a study which determined other factors that could influence how persuasive we are. They discovered that the persuasiveness of a speech depended on the perceived credibility of the speaker, how attractive they were, whether they were speaking first or last or if they were speaking to the ideal demographic for the related topic.

10. Language

Some words carry more impact than others. Using this understanding we can break persuasive speech up into three groups.

God - These words include terms which offer blessings, sacrifices, value or progress.

Devil - Words which are linked to negative connotations and make us feel disgust or bad. These include terms such as racist, rapist, evil, murder etc.

Charismatic - These words are more difficult to define in comparison to God and Devil words. Charismatic words are generally positive including terms such as giving, freedom, impressive and interesting.

The five most influential words in the English language are - New, free, You, Instantly and Because.

These top ten principles can be used as the basic building blocks for helping you develop a more persuasive personality in your career.

Chapter 8 - Mind Control in Love & Relationships

While we can be subjected to manipulation for any number of reasons, most manipulations tend to occur in relationships whether personal or professional.

Personal relationships are especially known for breeding emotional manipulators who can make the life of their partners unbearable. Being in a romantic relationship with a manipulator can become very damaging and should be avoided at all costs. It steadily wears down the victim's feelings of self-worth and can make them unwittingly compromise their personal values. This leads to a loss of self-respect and allows the manipulator to further remain in control.

If manipulation is used in relationship to terrorize, abuse or control, then the manipulator clearly has some psychological and emotional problems which need addressing. The desire to control another stems from a weak sense of self. If you feel you're in an abusive relationship, then get out as soon as you can.

Can You Make Someone Love You?

We fall in love by finding someone who we feel good being around. Someone whose basic values, beliefs, interests and background is in harmony with ours. Without being aware of it, when we meet someone we're attracted too, our subconscious automatically goes through a "checklist" and either marks this person as a potential romantic partner or someone to keep at arm's length. Unfortunately, many people's subconscious checklist doesn't run optimally and so we allow manipulators to slip through the net, especially since many appear to be charming and confident.

Using direct manipulation to influence someone into loving us is very unlikely. However, certain persuasion techniques can allow us to create an initial spark of interest and give us something to build upon.

The best way to draw others towards us is by working to boost our self-worth and esteem. Doing this can be as simple as changing our inner dialogue. Until we believe we're are desirable, intelligent and fascinating, we cannot expect anyone else to see us like that. When we feel good about ourselves, we increase our personal vibrations which then attracts love into our lives.

So, no, you can't manipulate someone into loving you, but there are many things you can do to increase your chances of being liked, appreciated and appealing. The rest is simply chemistry.

Manipulation in Love and Relationships

Persuasion can be successfully used in seeking relationships providing your intentions are pure and you would like to create a serious dialogue with someone. We can then begin to leverage whatever tools we have available to us.

In relationships, it's usually men who are known as the manipulators, but women also have their own means of controlling their partners.

Ways women manipulate men:

> ➤ *Pretend to be helpless, scared or weak*

Most men have this need to feel superior. Women know this and often use it to their advantage. By appearing fragile and helpless, they gain power as they're controlling how the man behaves in response. By simply making a man feel strong and needed helps draw them inwards and lower their guard in the midst of a weak female. But they are instead leaving themselves wide open to be exploited.

➤ *Pretend to be submissive*

Many women love using this technique to manipulate men. They do this by always agreeing with their partner, by letting him have the last word and by doing what he thinks is right. Although these may look like cheap tricks to keep their man happy, many a marriage has been saved by a woman's willingness to play the game of the weaker and more obedient partner.

➤ *Admiring and praising*

When women start praising their men excessively, the men should start to wonder why, although they rarely do. Men love being appreciated and admired by women, and this ego inflation often leaves them blind and vulnerable to be manipulated.

➤ *Crying*

A crying woman appears weak and defenseless and the man's first reaction is to hold and comfort her. A manipulative woman might use this to gain attention, to make a man feel guilty or as a form of blackmail. Sometimes, the only way to make her stop crying is to give in to her demands.

➤ Nagging

Nagging is annoying but incredibly effective. The best thing about it is that it can be so infuriating that most men sooner or later figure out it's better to do what they're been asked straight away than to undergo hours (or days, or weeks) of biting comments.

➤ Avoiding

Women turn to this tactic when nothing else seems to work. They get men to notice them by avoiding or ignoring them. Inexplicable silences and distance between partners or someone they're attracted too, sooner or later makes the man start considering the woman more. After an argument, some women won't talk for days (if they can help it), and most men will eventually cave in. Women play this card knowing that some people only sense the true value of something when they lose it. This mind game clearly sends the message – this is how your life would be without me.

➤ *The Art of Seduction*

This is likely the most well-known female manipulation tactic. We have all seen the movies where an attractive girl has the inert ability to flirt and seduce her male counterpart to get what she wants. Masterful female seducers usually have an array of tools at their disposal, the most effective one, of course, is the feminine body. Men are naturally more visual creatures and are easily influenced by something that's 'easy on the eye'. By simply revealing a little flesh, or giving him the flirtiest look, can be misinterpreted at the possibility of attraction. This is often all it takes to grab a man's attention and leave him wide open for manipulation.

Men and Dating

It is not uncommon for some women to worry about men using a trick on them to increase attraction. However, attraction is not something which can be faked. Attraction is natural. A woman cannot stop herself from being attracted to a man regardless of whether he's 'her type' or not. Mind control tricks and NLP techniques to trick women into liking you are not sustainable, eventually the trick will wear off. Instead work on developing your confidence, self-worth, appearance and personality. When a man is living from his true authenticity that is when he is the most appealing to the opposite sex. There's nothing more he needs to do except learn how to live from his heart. Then almost every woman he meets will view him in the way he intends.

However, for those of you who still desire to learn certain strategies. Here are some techniques, purely for educational purposes. I do not endorse or promote the use of such behaviors.

1) Keep her guessing

The next time you're attracted to a woman, instead of making your intentions obvious, conceal your true feelings. The understanding behind this philosophy is - what a woman can't detect, she can't reject. So, don't be too upfront with the woman of your desires. Most people (men and women) enjoy a challenge and usually see whatever comes easily of lower value. But when we have to earn something, we gain a higher degree of satisfaction from it. Make her earn your attention. You can also use the 'push-pull' technique, here you would show interest in her but then withdraw. You're effectively drawing her towards you but then pushing her away.

2) Act interested in her

This step is contradictory to the first step. But this tactic is best deployed once you have her attention and you're maybe even dating. Take her out to nice restaurants, treat her well and pay for everything. The aim is to help her feel safe and comfortable in your presence. But never disclose to her you like her. That next step may seem a little extreme but now you must stop communicating with her for no reason. Cut all contact with her. This means not answering her calls or responding to any of her texts. When you do finally reply, you tell her something like 'I don't think this will work out, let's just be friends'. This will drive her crazy!! From here on in, she will work to seduce you and she'll want you even more. The aim here isn't to abuse or harm anyone but to help increase attraction.

3) The Jealousy Game

Inciting jealousy in a woman can be incredibly powerful in increasing her attraction towards you. Jealously has the power to make people act irrationally. When people become irrational their psychology loses its state of balance which makes them more susceptible to manipulation. So by making a woman jealous you'll be able to manipulate her into going out with you. Although jealously can bring out strong emotions in people please use this tactic with care or steer clear of it altogether.

If you do use this, make her jealous by mentioning other women you're interested in, this will make you seem more appealing. Women are naturally drawn to the popular guy and will gladly compete with other females to win him over. This goes back to early evolutionary times, where women's survival was often based on being within a community and social groups to feel safe. This naturally draws her to the social guy, as she believes her needs will be met and she'll be looked after.

4) Conditioning

This is a tool which can take more time to implement but is powerful in helping influence a woman into liking you.

The process itself is simple to do. It involves rewarding her when she pleases you or does something you approve of. But withdrawing your attention and focusing on other women when she does something you disapprove of. This 'stick and carrot' approach will make her more likely to do the things which please you more often.

These strategies have been included for educational purposes only. No offense is intended.

Conclusion

Using manipulation and persuasion tactics can help us improve various aspects of our lives. There is a darkness and unknown attached to this area when we consider how mind control is used in its extremities.

By being clear of your motives for using such techniques we can start to enrich our lives. Its not the method which is bad or evil but the person who uses them. Perhaps you've learnt how to be more influential in your business or relationships. But whatever your motives go into this with a clear conscience and all will be well. When done in the right way, everyone wins.

Thank you!

References

https://www.fastcompany.com/3030173/how-to-use-10-psychological-theories-to-persuade-people
https://copyhackers.com/2014/04/website-persuasion/

https://en.wikipedia.org/wiki/James_Vicary

http://www.nytimes.com/2007/07/31/health/psychology/31subl.html?ei=5090&en=62f9b092a91bc6dc&ex=1343534400&partner=rssuserland&emc=rss&pagewanted=all

"Lifton's Brainwashing Processes." ChangingMinds. http://changingminds.org/techniques/conversion/lifton_brainwashing.htm

How to Win Friends and Influence People Paperback – 6 Apr 2006 by Dale Carnegie (Author)

Made in the USA
Middletown, DE
13 May 2018